baby

baby Jesus

basket

Bible

birds

cloud

coat

cross

desert

Do not

eyes

feet

fire

fish

flies

hair

hand

happy

heaven

house

light

lion

love

mad

man

money

people

Pharaoh

pray

rain

right

river

sheep

shepherd

sick

sing

snake

strong

sun

temple

tomb

treasure

water

wind

woman

world

worship

wrong

Presented to

_____

By _____

On _____

Picture That!

Bible Storybook

Written by
Tracy Harrast

Illustrated by
Garry Colby

Picture That!

Bible Storybook

Over 65 Stories

ZondervanPublishingHouse

Grand Rapids, Michigan

A Division of HarperCollinsPublishers

Dedication

For 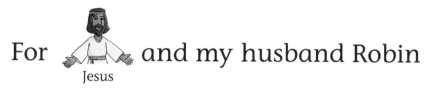 and my husband Robin
Jesus

who fill my  with .
world   love

Library of Congress Catalog Card Number: 97–61399

Published by Zondervan Publishing House
Grand Rapids, MI 49530, U.S.A
http://www.zondervan.com
Printed in the United States of America
All rights reserved

98 99 00 01 02 03 04 ❖ 12 11 10 9 8 7 6 5 4 3

RRD

A Note to Moms & Dads

The first time you travel through this book with your children, you may need to be the one who reads the text and a few of the captions. Next time, just sit back and be the audience! Your children will be thrilled by how easy it is to read to *you* for a change.

The truth identified after each story helps your children think beyond details of the story to what it teaches. Emphasize that there are many lessons to learn from each Bible event. In fact, the Holy Spirit can teach us additional truths every time we reread a Bible story.

Reading with you may be your children's best memories. So lift them onto your lap and enjoy helping them get to know God by reading these stories adapted from his holy Word.

Tracy L. Harrast

Table of Contents

Old Testament

New Testament

 The Start of the World

Genesis 1

Long ago God said, "Let there be

," and there was .

light   light

The next day he made the

sky. On the **3**rd day, God made

dry , plants, , and

ground   flowers

. The **4**th day he put the

trees

 and   in the sky.

sun   moon   up

On the **5**th day, God made that

fish

2

swim in the  and  that fly

water   birds

in the sky. He made more

animals and then a and a

man

 on the 6th day. All that he

woman

made was very good.

What Did You Learn?
God made the world!

The First Man and Woman

Genesis 2:7–8, 18, 22–25

The very **1**st 👤 (man) was Adam. God made

him out of the dust of the 🌱 (ground).

Adam lived in a pretty 🌳 (garden). It was

called the 🌳 (Garden) of Eden. God said, "It is

not good for the 👤 (man) to be alone." So God

made a 👩 (woman) to be with him. Her name

was Eve. Adam and Eve were 🙂 (happy).

4

What Did You Learn?

God does not want
us to feel alone.

A Snake Lies to Eve

Genesis 3:1–6, 23

God told Adam and Eve, " (Do not)  (eat) the fruit from the (tree) in the middle of the (garden)." The devil turned into the shape of a (snake) and talked to Eve. He told Eve it was good to  (eat) the fruit from that (tree). The (snake) was lying! But Eve believed him. She chose to (eat) the fruit and then

gave some to Adam to . God was
eat

 because they did not obey him. So
sad

Adam and Eve had to leave

the  .
garden

What Did You Learn?
The devil tells lies.

Noah Makes an Ark

Genesis 6—7

God told a man named Noah that it would

 rain so long that water would cover the

whole world. God told Noah to make an

 ark and to bring **2** of every animal into

it. Noah did what God said. Then rain

fell for **40** days. It covered the world with

 water. But Noah, his family, and the

animals were safe in the ark.

8

What Did You Learn?

We need to do what God says.

Look at the Stars

Genesis 15:5–6; 18:10–12; 21:1–3

God told a  named Abraham to look

up at the 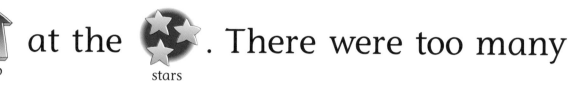. There were too many

to count! God said Abraham would

have that many  in

his family. Abraham

believed what God

said. Abraham's

wife was Sarah. When

she heard that she would have

a , she laughed. She was an old

baby

. How could she have a ? But God

woman   baby

kept his promise. When Sarah was **90**

years old, she had a named Isaac.

baby

What Did You Learn?

God keeps his promises.

A Wife for Isaac

Genesis 24:1–28

Isaac had grown to be a man . His dad sent

a servant to find a woman that Isaac could

marry. The servant stopped to pray at a

well. The servant said to God, "I will ask a

 woman for a drink . If she says, 'I will give

 water to your camels too,' let her be

the one you want for Isaac." Then

the servant saw Rebekah. He asked

her for a . Rebekah said she

drink

would give to his

water

camels

too. So the knew God

servant

wanted her to marry Isaac!

What Did You Learn?

If we pray, we can know
what God wants.

Bad, Mad Brothers

Genesis 37:3–4, 23–33

An old  man named Israel had **12** sons.

He liked Joseph the most. He gave

Joseph a beautiful, fancy coat . This

made Joseph's brothers mad .

They wanted a fancy coat

too! They took Joseph's

 coat and then threw him down

into a well. The well was

14

empty. There wasn't any  in it.
water

Then Joseph's brothers pulled him
up

out of the well and sold him as a .
servant

They made it look like animals ate

Joseph. They were bad brothers!

What Did You Learn?

Be happy when good things
happen to others, not mad like
Joseph's bad brothers.

Joseph Forgives

Genesis 39:20; 41:39–57; 43; 45:1–21

Joseph was put in . He got out by

helping know what his dreams
Pharaoh

meant. gave Joseph a job making
Pharaoh

sure in saved food for
people   Egypt

the time when

16

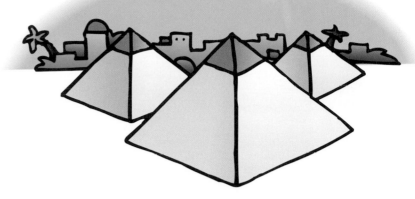

it would not

grow. Later, Joseph's

brothers came to 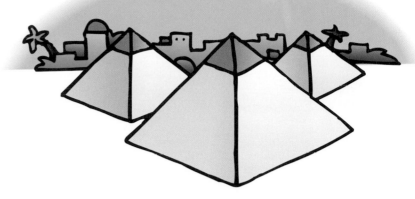 to buy food to

Egypt

. Joseph forgave them for throwing

eat

him ⬇ into a well and for selling him

down

as a 🧍. He gave them food to and

servant   eat

let them live in .

Egypt

What Did You Learn?
We need to forgive others.

A Baby Floats in a Basket

Exodus 2:1–10

Bad wanted to harm boys.

Pharaoh

baby

But God had a plan for a boy

baby

named Moses. The baby's mom hid

Moses to keep him safe from bad .

Pharaoh

When she couldn't hide him anymore,

she put her in a . Then she

baby

basket

put the in a . Moses'

basket

river

sister watched to

18

be sure he was safe. The

 floated in the . A
basket   river

princess found the in the
                                baby

. She raised Moses as
basket   baby

her own son. And he was safe

from bad .
                Pharaoh

What Did You Learn?

God has a plan
for our life.

19

God Talks From a Bush

Exodus 3:1–21

The
Israelites were from Joseph's family.

The
people in Egypt were mean to the

Israelites. They made them be their

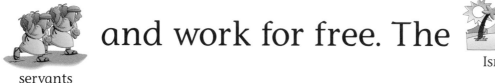
servants and work for free. The
Israelites

were
sad. They prayed for

God to help them get out

of
Egypt. God heard

20

them . So he spoke to Moses, who

was now a grown 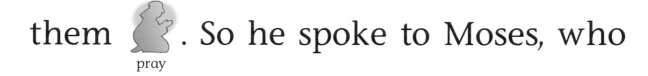, from a bush that

was on ! He told Moses to get the

 out of . God said to tell

 to let the  .

What Did You Learn?

God hears us when we pray.

Pharaoh Says No

Exodus 7:14–25; 8; 9:22–23;
10:21–23; 12:31

Moses told to let the  leave
Pharaoh   Israelites

 or bad things would happen.
Egypt

But said no. He would not let
Pharaoh

the . So the turned
Israelites   go   river

red. There were too many
frogs

and . Little lumps of ice
flies

called hail fell from the sky.
down

It was as dark as for **3** days.

night

But said no again and again.

Pharaoh

He tried to God's plan to let

stop

the  . After **10** bad

Israelites go

things happened, at last

 let the .

Pharaoh Israelites go

What Did You Learn?

No one can stop
God's plans.

23

God Splits the Water

Exodus 13:18–22; 14

God led the Israelites through the desert.

They followed a cloud during the day

and  fire at night.  Pharaoh wanted the

 Israelites to come back to  Egypt. He and

his  army chased them! The  Israelites

could not cross the Red Sea. So God

made the water split! The Israelites could

 walk through on dry  ground. They got

away from Pharaoh and his  army!

What Did You Learn?

God gets us through our troubles.

God Feeds the Israelites

Exodus 15:22–25; 16:1—17:7

While the  Israelites were in the  desert,

they wanted to drink some water. But the

 water was bad. One time God showed

Moses a piece of wood to throw in the

 water to make it good. Another time God made

26

water come out of a rock . God sent

food to eat too. He sent  birds called

quail and bread from  heaven called

manna for them to 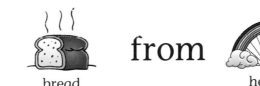 eat . The manna

tasted sweet like honey. The  Israelites

found it on the ground each morning.

What Did You Learn?
God gives us what we need.

27

The Ten Com

Exodus 19:20; 20:1–17

God wrote **10** rules for how to live. We call

them the  . God gave the to Moses

10 Commandments · · · · · · · 10 Commandments

1. Put God **1**st. Do not love anyone or anything more than God.

2. Do not make a statue of another god or worship other gods.

3. Do not misuse the name of the LORD.

4. Keep the Sabbath day holy. Do not work on that day.

28

on a . They are ways to show for

mountain   love

God and for . This is what they say:

people

5. Honor your father and mother.

6. Do not kill.

7. If you get married, be true to your husband or wife.

8. Do not steal.

9. Do not lie.

10. Do not want what other have.

people

What Did You Learn?

Keeping the **10** Commandments shows that we love God and people.

29

A Wall Falls Down

Joshua 6:1–20

There was a wall around the city of

Jericho. God told Joshua how to knock

 down the wall so his  army could go

inside. The  army marched around

the city once a day for **6** days. Some

 men called priests carried

 trumpets. On the **7**th day,

the army marched

around the  7 times.

city

The priests blew the .

trumpets

When the heard the

army

, all the shouted.

trumpets   men

Then the fell !

wall   down

What Did You Learn?

God can knock down
our problems.

The Sun and Moon Stop

Joshua 10:7–20

Joshua and his (army) had to fight

another (army). God told Joshua, " (Do not)

be (afraid) of them. I have handed them

over to you." Joshua told the (sun) and

the (moon) to stand still. God made the

 and the   in the

middle of the sky! The did

not  until about a day later. God

helped Joshua and his army win!

What Did You Learn?

We can win if God is on our side.

God Makes Samson Strong

Judges 13:1–5; 14:6; 16:15–20, 28–30

An angel said Samson should *never*

cut his hair. God made Samson strong.

He was so strong that he killed a lion

with his hands! When bad

 men found out what made

Samson strong, they cut his

 hair and put him in jail.

Samson was not  strong

34

anymore. He began to . He prayed

that God would make him one

more time. God did! Samson made a

whole building fall .

What Did You Learn?

God can make
us strong.

God Talks to Samuel

1 Samuel 3

Samuel lived with a priest named

Eli. Samuel was Eli's helper. After the

 sun went down one night , Samuel heard a

voice call his name. He thought it was Eli.

He got up to see what Eli wanted. Eli

said, "I didn't call you. Now go back and

lie down ." Samuel went back and lay down .

He heard the voice a **2ⁿᵈ** time. He got up

36

again. But it wasn't Eli, so Samuel went to lie  down again. After this happened the 3rd time that night, Eli told Samuel it must be God. God called, "Samuel!" Samuel said, "Speak. I'm listening." Then God talked to him!

What Did You Learn?

God wants us to listen to him.

David Fights a Giant

1 Samuel 17:1–50

Everyone in an  was of a
army   afraid

 named Goliath. He was more than
giant

9 feet tall! But a boy named David
shepherd

was not . He knew God helped
afraid

him before, and he knew God

would help him again. David

put a in a sling and
stone

spun it around. The
stone

hit the  giant on his forehead.

The  giant fell  down. David

won!

What Did You Learn?

No problem
is too big for God.

Wise Solomon

1 Kings 3:5–15; 4:32–34

In a dream, God told a king named

Solomon, "Ask for anything you want

me to give you." King

Solomon asked God for

wisdom to know right from

 wrong . This made God happy .

He gave Solomon the wisdom

he wanted, and he gave him

and riches too. Many from

money   people

around the came to hear

world   King

Solomon. Many of his wise sayings

are in the .

Bible

What Did You Learn?

God helps us know what
is right and what is wrong.

Who Makes the Rain?

1 Kings 16:29–33; 17:1–6

A  king named Ahab believed in a

pretend god that was a 📿 statue. He thought

the 📿 statue made it 🌧 rain. The 👑 king started to

🙏 worship this pretend god. This made the

real God really 😠 mad. Elijah told the king

about the real God. But the king

continued to  worship the 📿 statue. So God did not let 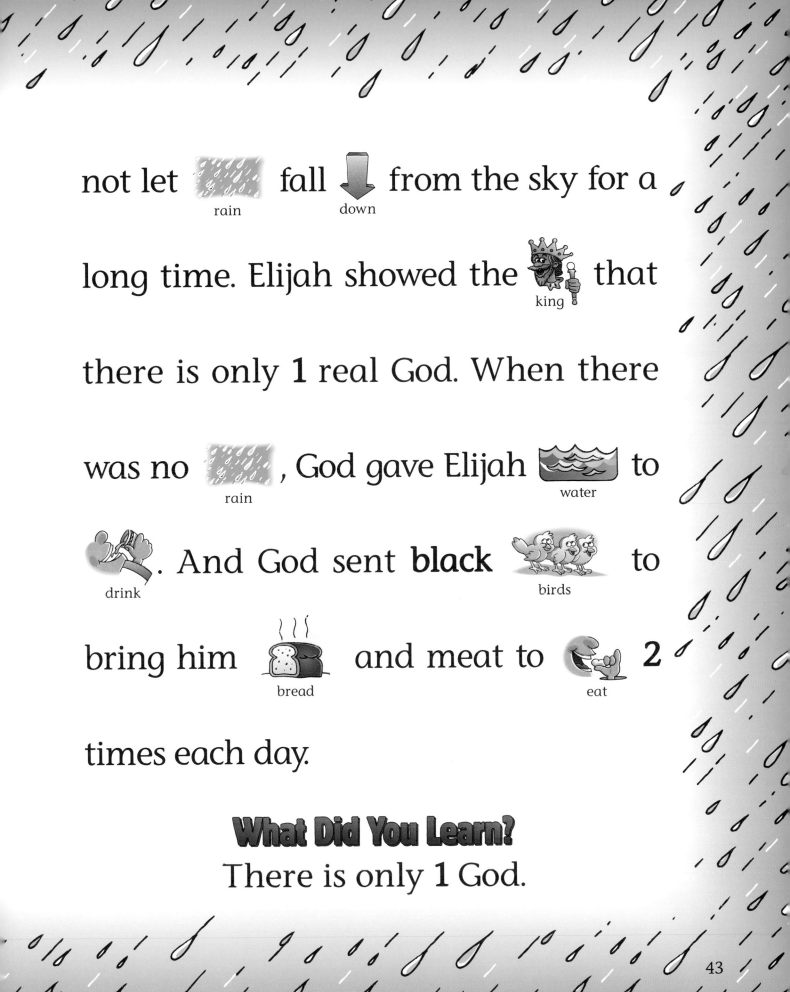 rain fall ↓ down from the sky for a

long time. Elijah showed the king that

there is only **1** real God. When there

was no rain , God gave Elijah water to

drink . And God sent **black** birds to

bring him bread and meat to eat **2**

times each day.

What Did You Learn?
There is only **1** God.

Elijah's Trip to Heaven

2 Kings 2:1–15

A named Elisha wanted to work for

God like his friend Elijah did. One day

Elijah rolled his and hit the

 with it. The  split and the **2**

 could across. Then a chariot

and horses of 🔥 took Elijah ⬆ to

🌈 in a great 💨. Elisha picked

⬆ Elijah's 🧥 that had fallen to the

 ground . He hit the river

with it and God made

the river split again. This

showed Elisha that he

would work for God—just

like Elijah had!

What Did You Learn?

It is good to want to work for God.

45

Sing to God!

Psalms 8:3; 23:1; 24:1; 68:32

 David wrote songs to God called "psalms." The king sang these words:

"God takes care of me. God hears me when I pray. The LORD is my shepherd.

I will not be afraid of my enemies. I think about

the moon and  stars.

God's hands have made

the . I will praise him with all my

world

heart. Come and to God, you

sing

kingdoms of the ."

world

What Did You Learn?

God likes for us
to sing praise to him
like King David did.

Three Men Stand in a Fire

Daniel 3

A (king) said that (people) must  (worship) a big (statue). If they didn't, they would be thrown

into a (fire). 3  (men) would not  (worship) the

 (statue). They would only (worship) the real

God. They did what was (right). The (king)

had them thrown into a (fire). But the

 (fire) did not burn the 3 men. God kept

them safe!

What Did You Learn?

It's better to obey God
rather than people.

A Hand Writes on a Wall

Daniel 5

A bad king had a party with his friends.

They knew it was 👎 wrong to 🥤 drink out of

cups from God's 🏛 temple. But they did it

anyway. Then the fingers of a ✋ hand

appeared. They wrote

strange words on a 🧱 wall.

They wrote **M E N E** and

more letters. The king was

so  that his

afraid

face turned white and

he fell ⬇. Later, Daniel told him

down

what the words on the 🧱 said:

wall

God would not let the 👑 be a 👑

king   king

anymore.

What Did You Learn?

God has more power than kings.

Lions Skip Dinner

Daniel 6:11–22

A (king) wouldn't let (people) (pray) to the real

God. He said they could only (pray) to him,

the (king). But Daniel would not (pray) to the

 (king). He would only pray to the real God.

He did not let anyone STOP (stop) him

from doing

what was right.

The  king sent Daniel to stay all night in a

den with lions ! But God kept Daniel

safe. God sent an angel to hold the lions'

mouths shut. The lions did not hurt

Daniel at all!

What Did You Learn?

Do what is right, even
when people try to stop us.

A Big Fish Swallows Jonah

Jonah 1—2

God told a named Jonah to to the

man   go

 of Nineveh. But Jonah tried to

city

run away from God. He got on a . God

boat

sent a that almost made the

storm   boat

sink. The on the threw Jonah

men   boat

into the so the would . A

water   storm   stop

big swallowed Jonah. **3** days later it

fish

spit him onto dry . Then Jonah

ground

went where God wanted him to .

go

What Did You Learn?

We need to go where God wants us to go.

Testament

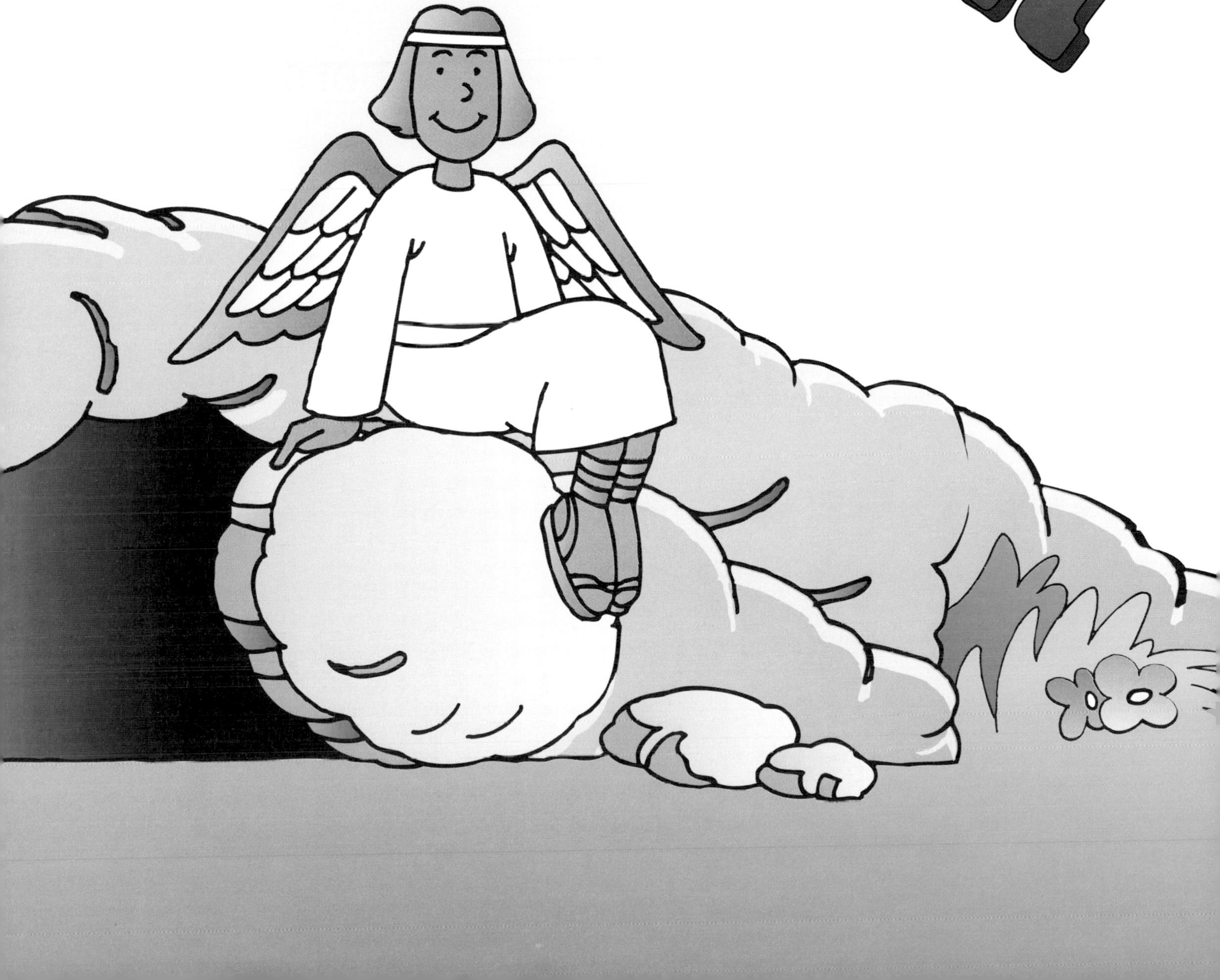

Baby Jesus Is Born

Luke 1:26–32; 2:6–16

An told Mary she would have a
angel

 named . He was the Son of God!
baby   Jesus

When was ready to be born, Mary
baby Jesus

and Joseph were far from their . The
house

 was full, so they stayed in a stable.
inn

They laid in a manger.
baby Jesus

Some  were watching their in a

shepherds

sheep

field nearby that . An  told the

night

angel

 that the one who would save them

shepherds

was born. So they came to see .

baby Jesus

What Did You Learn?

Jesus is the Son of God.

Wise Men Follow the Star

Matthew 2:1–2, 9–11

Wise Men wanted to

worship

baby Jesus
. When

they saw a big
star   up

in the sky, they knew it

would lead them to .
baby Jesus

The came to a above the place
star   stop

where was. The Wise Men bowed
baby Jesus

 to worship baby Jesus.

Then they opened

their  and gave

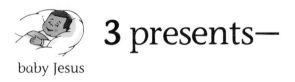 **3** presents—

gold, incense, and a

spice called myrrh.

What Did You Learn?

Wise people worship Jesus.

Where's Jesus?

Luke 2:41–52

When 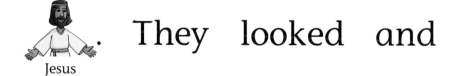 was **12** years old, Mary and

Joseph took him to the (temple). On the way

back to their (house), Mary

and Joseph could not find

 (Jesus). They looked and

looked. **3** days later they

found (Jesus) in the (temple). He

was talking with teachers

62

and asking questions. He amazed them with what he understood about God and about what the 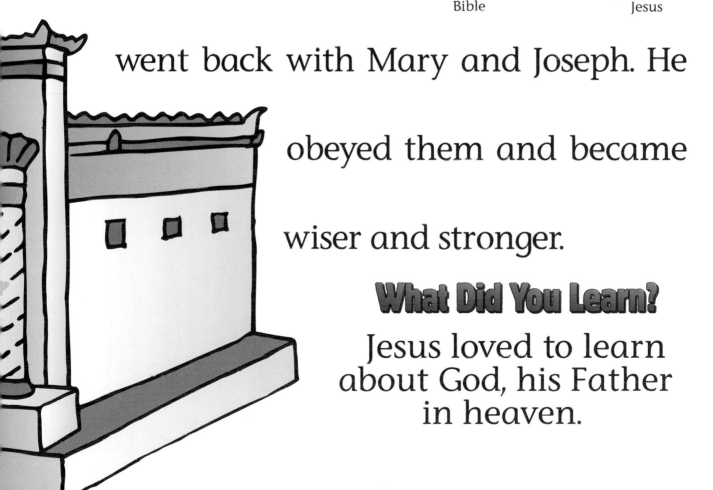 says.

Bible

Jesus

went back with Mary and Joseph. He obeyed them and became wiser and stronger.

What Did You Learn?

Jesus loved to learn about God, his Father in heaven.

Jesus Is Baptized

Matthew 3:13–17
(see also Mark 1:1–11; Luke 3:1–22)

John baptized . He put

people

them in the to show

water

that God would wash away

their sins because of .

Jesus

 never did anything

Jesus

, but he said he must

wrong

be baptized too. So John

baptized and then came

up

out of the . At that moment

water   heaven

was opened, and the Spirit of God came

 on him like a dove. A voice from

down

 said, "This is my Son, and I

heaven   love

him. I am very pleased with him."

What Did You Learn?

God is happy when we
are baptized.

Jesus Does Not Sin

Matthew 4:1–10 (see also Luke 4:1–13)

After Jesus was baptized, he went into

the  desert. For **40** days and **40**

nights Jesus did not 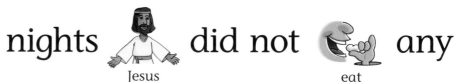 eat any

food. The devil tried to get

 Jesus to turn stones into

 bread. He tried to get

 Jesus to jump down from the

top of a temple. The devil

took to a very high . He showed

Jesus

mountain

him all the kingdoms of the . And he

world

tried to get to him. Those

Jesus

worship

things were  ! would not do

wrong

Jesus

them. said no to the devil by telling

Jesus

him what God says in the .

Bible

What Did You Learn?

Learning Bible verses helps us say no to the devil.

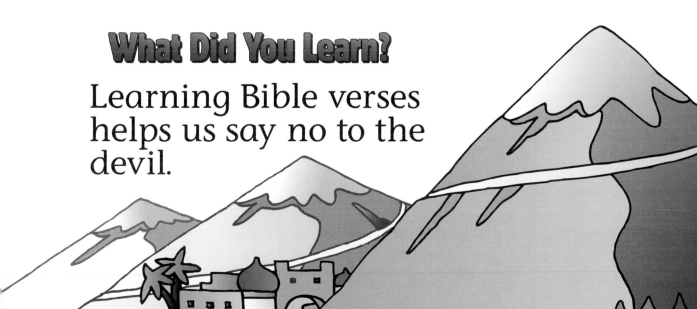

How to Go

John 3:16,

 said need to

Jesus   people

trust him as the only way to

God the Father. He said, "I am

the way and the truth and the life.

No one comes to the Father except

through me." said God

Jesus

had so much for the

love

to Heaven

36; 14:6

world that he gave his **1** and

only Son. Whoever believes in

Jesus will live forever in heaven.

But those who say no to Jesus will

not.

What Did You Learn?

Jesus is the only way to get
to our Father in heaven.

Following Jesus

Matthew 4:18–20; 9:9; 10:39; 16:25;
(see also Mark 8:35; Luke 9:24)

Jesus

asked

people

to follow him.

Jesus

had **12** special helpers called disciples

who did that. Some were

fishermen like Peter and

James and John who left

their fish and

their nets and

70

their to follow . One
boats · Jesus · man

named Matthew used to collect .
money

But he also went to follow . He
Jesus

became one of the **12** disciples too.

 said whoever follows him will
Jesus

live with him forever in .
heaven

What Did You Learn?

Jesus wants us to follow him.

Jesus Fills Boats With Fish

Luke 5:1–11

 told Peter to take his into deep

Jesus · boat

 and let 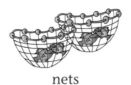 to catch .

water · down · nets · fish

"We did not catch any all ," Peter

night

said, "But because you say so, I will let

down

the ." They caught so many

nets · fish

that they filled **2** ! Then said

boats · Jesus

that instead of bringing into a ,

fish · boat

they would help bring to .

people · Jesus

72

Jesus Heals Many People

Matthew 8:14–17; 9:27–30;
Mark 3:1–5; 8:22–25; John 5:1–9

Jesus cared about people who were sick.

He healed eyes that couldn't see and

legs that couldn't walk. He healed

people who could not hear or talk. He

made someone's hand better. He made a

fever go down. Jesus said faith in God was

what healed those people.

What Did You Learn?

Jesus can make sick
people well.

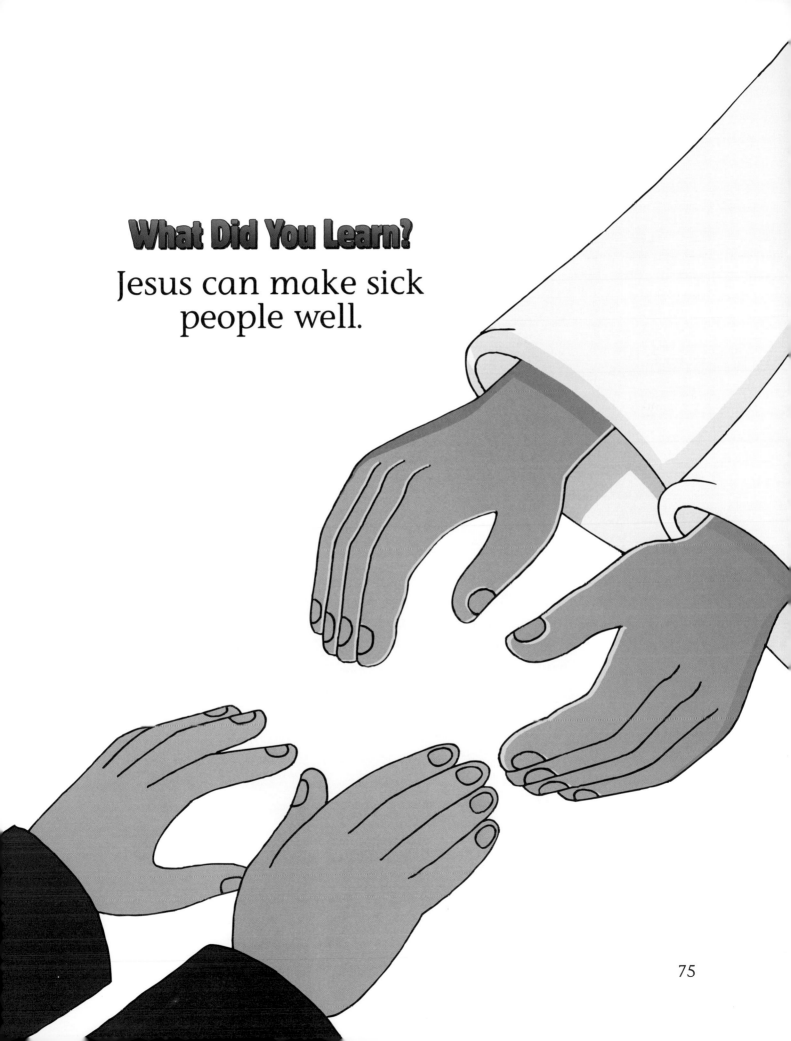

A Hole in the Roof

Mark 2:1–5, 12

A who could not had **4** friends.

man   walk

They carried him to a where

house   Jesus

was teaching. The was full of !

house   people

They could not get to . So the man's

Jesus

4 friends made a hole in the and

roof

lowered him to . When he saw

down   Jesus

their faith, forgave the man's sins

Jesus

and healed him. He could !

walk

76

What Did You Learn?

We can help our friends get to Jesus.

Jesus Talks From a Mountain

Matthew 5:1–12
(see also Luke 6:17–26)

 Jesus taught people from the side of a

 mountain. Jesus said that even when life is

hard in this world, believers are blessed

because we will go to  heaven. Those

who are sad will be comforted. Those

who forgive will be forgiven. If people are

 mad at us because we love Jesus, we can

be  anyway because we will get a

great reward in heaven.

What Did You Learn?
We are blessed.

Be Like Salt and Light

Matthew 5:13–16

 said we are the of the .
Jesus | salt | world

Like makes food taste better,
salt | Jesus

wants us to make the better. He
world

said we are the of the . He
light | world

wants us to let know we follow
people

him. said to let our shine in
Jesus | light

front of so they may see the good
people

we do and praise our Father in  .
heaven

80

What Did You Learn?

We can help make the world better.

Giving to Others

Matthew 5:42; 6:1–4; Luke 16:19–26

 Jesus said to give to people

who ask. He said not to turn

away from people who want to

borrow. He told about a rich man who

did not even give tiny pieces of

 bread to a hungry beggar to

 eat. Jesus said to give to

other 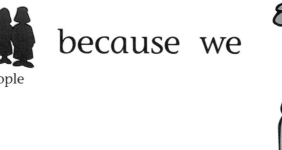 people because we

82

 love them, not so

that  people will see us

give and say we are

good. He said to give to

other  people because it is the  right

thing to do.

What Did You Learn?

Jesus wants us
to share.

How to Pray

Matthew 6:9–15

 Jesus showed his disciples how to pray.

He wants us to pray this way too. **1**st we

praise God in  heaven and tell him that

we want everyone to follow him as king.

Then we tell him we want things done

in the world the way he wants, just

as they are in  heaven. Next we ask for

 bread or whatever we need to eat

84

each day. And we ask God to forgive us

like we forgive other . If we do, our
people

Father in will also forgive us.
heaven

Last of all we ask him to keep us from

wanting to do what is .
wrong

What Did You Learn?

Jesus wants us
to pray like he did.

Do Not Worry

Matthew 6:25–33

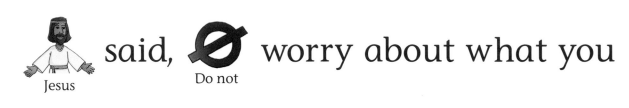 said,  worry about what you

will  or what you will wear. God

feeds the (birds) and he dresses the

(flowers) in nicer clothes than a (king) would

wear! (Jesus) said that we matter even

more than (birds) and (flowers)! All we

need to do is follow (Jesus) and try to be

like him. God will take care of the rest.

86

What Did You Learn?

God takes care of birds and flowers. He'll take care of us too!

A House on Rock and a House on Sand

Matthew 7:24–27

 Jesus says whoever obeys him is like a

 man who builds his house on the  rock.

The rain comes down. The  water rises up.

The 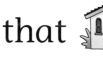 wind blows and beats against

that house. But it does not fall down. But

whoever does *not* obey is like a man who

builds his house on sand. The rain

comes . The rises . The

down water up

 blows and beats against that

wind

. And that falls with a

house house down

crash!

What Did You Learn?

If we obey Jesus, we will be strong like a house that will not fall down.

The Kingdom of Heaven

Matthew 13:32, 44–47

The  who follow as

people · Jesus

 are part of the kingdom of

king

. said the kingdom of

heaven · Jesus

 is like a tiny seed that grows

heaven

 to be a big . The come to

up · tree · birds

rest in its branches. It's like a that

net

catches many . The kingdom

fish

of is like a

heaven

pearl that is worth

a lot of . It's like

money

finding a hidden !

treasure

What Did You Learn?

If we follow Jesus as our king, we belong to the kingdom of heaven.

Jesus Stops a Storm

Matthew 8:23–27 (see also
Mark 4:35–41; Luke 8:22–25)

 was asleep in a when a
Jesus
boat
storm

started. The howled and the
wind

 crashed over the . Jesus'
water
boat

disciples were they would drown.
afraid

They woke . He said if they had
Jesus

more faith that they wouldn't be so .
afraid

Then told the and the
Jesus
wind

 to be still. That made the .
water
storm   stop

92

What Did You Learn?

Jesus has more power than the wind and the water.

Jesus Heals a Woman

*Luke 8:42–48 (see also
Matthew 9:20–22; Mark 5:24–34)*

Jesus

was walking in a crowd of
people
. He

came to a quick
stop
and asked, "Who

touched me?" A
woman
fell
down
at his
feet
.

She was very
afraid
. She was the one who

had reached out her
hand

to
Jesus
. She had been

sick
for **12** years.

She knew if she

94

touched , even

just the bottom edge of

his clothes, that she

would get better. said,

"Dear , don't give up hope. Your faith

has healed you."

What Did You Learn?

Jesus can help us when
we reach out to him.

Jesus Feeds a Crowd

John 6:1–14 (see also Matthew 14:15–21; Mark 6:30–44; Luke 9:10–17)

After spoke one day, a crowd of

 was hungry and wanted to

people   Jesus

give them something to

. One boy had **5**

eat

loaves of and

bread

2 . It didn't

fish

seem like it was

enough for everyone, but he gave Jesus

all he had. Jesus thanked God for the

 bread and fish . He broke the food

apart and gave it to the crowd of people

to eat . **5,000** men ate bread and fish

that day. Many women and  children also ate.

There were even **12**  of leftovers!
baskets

What Did You Learn?
Jesus cares about hungry people.

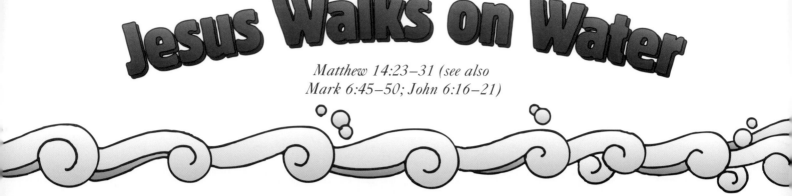

Jesus Walks on Water

Matthew 14:23–31 (see also
Mark 6:45–50; John 6:16–21)

The disciples were in a on a lake.
boat

 took a on out to the
Jesus   walk   water

! When they saw , they were .
boat   Jesus   afraid

But he said, "It is I.  be ." let
Do not   afraid   Jesus

Peter  on the too. But then
walk   water

Peter took his off of . He
eyes   Jesus

98

looked at the wind and felt afraid . He

started to go down into the  water , but Jesus

reached out his hand and caught him. He

said Peter needed more faith.

What Did You Learn?

Faith in Jesus helps us
not to be afraid.

A Samaritan Helps

Luke 10:30–37

 Jesus told about a **man** who was hurt by

robbers. **2** **men** passed by him. They did

not **stop** to help. Then a Samaritan saw

the **man**. He put the **man** on his **donkey** and

took him

to an

inn.

100

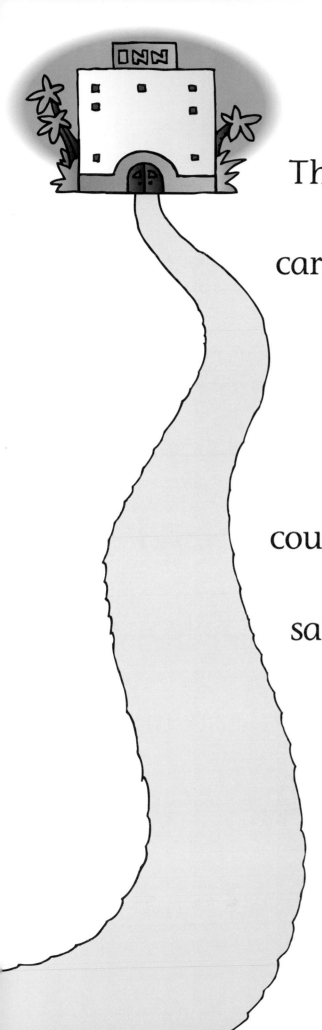

There the Samaritan took care of the
man
. Then he gave
money
to the owner of the
inn
so the hurt
man
could stay there longer.
Jesus
said to love others like the good Samaritan did.

What Did You Learn?

We need to stop and help people.

Mary Listens to Jesus

Luke 10:38–42

 went to stay at Martha's .

Martha had a sister named Mary. While

 talked, Mary sat at his  and

listened. Martha was busy working.

She said to , "Tell Mary to help me."

 said, "You are worried and upset

about many things. But only **1** thing

is needed. Mary has chosen what is

better." It was better to sit  and listen

down

to .

Jesus

What Did You Learn?

We shouldn't ever be
too busy to sit down and
learn about Jesus.

One Lost Sheep

Luke 15:3–7

 Jesus

told a story

about a shepherd who had

100 sheep . When **1**

was missing, the shepherd

left all the other sheep and went to

look for it. When the shepherd found the **1**

 sheep , he carried it back on his shoulders

and had a party. Jesus said  angels will

be  like that when a person who

went away from God comes back to

him again.

What Did You Learn?

Jesus loves every **1** of us!

A Forgiving Dad

Luke 15:11–24

 Jesus told a story about a son who

asked his dad for lots of money . The son

left his dad's house and he spent all his

 money on wrong things. The son

was afraid his dad would not want

him to come back because he had

been so bad. But he decided to go

back anyway. His dad was very

 to see him. He was

filled with great

love

for his son. He ran to his

son and gave him a hug

and a kiss!

What Did You Learn?

When we do wrong things, our Father in heaven still loves us.

Jesus Brings People to Life

John 11:17–45

Mary and Martha had a brother named Lazarus. They were very sad because he died. Jesus was very sad too.

He went to the  tomb where Lazarus was buried. He said to open the  tomb. Jesus looked up and prayed. Then he said, "Lazarus, come out!" The man who had been dead began to walk out of

the !   brought other dead

tomb   Jesus

 back to life on other days too. He

people

said, "I am the resurrection and the life.

Whoever believes in me will live, even if

they die."

What Did You Learn?

If we believe in Jesus, we will
live again even if we die.

Children Go to Jesus

Matthew 19:13–15 (see also Matthew 18:3;
Mark 10:13–16; Luke 18:15–17)

Some people brought little children to Jesus.

They wanted Jesus to put his hands on

them and pray for them. The disciples

told the people to stop. But  Jesus said, "Let

the little children come to me. Do not keep

them away. The kingdom of  heaven

belongs to people like them." Jesus said

that in his kingdom are like

people

 . took the

children   Jesus

 in his arms. Then

children

he placed his on

hands

them and blessed them.

What Did You Learn?

Jesus loves children.

A Little Man in a Tree

Luke 19:1–10

Zacchaeus wanted to see Jesus. But he was

too short! He could not see over the people!

So he climbed up a tree. When Jesus saw

the man in the tree, he said, "Zacchaeus,

come down at once. I must stay at your

 house today." Jesus helped Zacchaeus

want to do what was right. He said he'd

give back money he had gotten the wrong way.

112

What Did You Learn?

When Jesus comes into our life,
we want to do what is right.

Jesus Comes As a King

Matthew 21:1–11 (see also Mark 11:1–11; Luke 19:28–44; John 12:12–19)

In times, a rode a horse into

a when there was war. And a

rode a when there was peace.

rode a  into a to show that

he was a of peace. The spread

their and palm branches on

the for to ride across. They

praised God for the miracles they had

seen 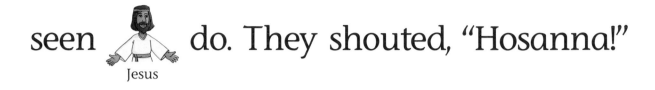 do. They shouted, "Hosanna!"

Jesus

That means "Save us!"

What Did You Learn?

Jesus is the king of peace.

The Most Important Commandment

Matthew 22:34–40
(see also Mark 12:28–31)

Someone asked Jesus

which of God's rules is the

most important. Jesus

said the **1**st and greatest

commandment is to  love the

Lord your God with all your heart,

soul, and mind. He said the **2**nd

commandment is to
love

other like you
people   love

yourself. said all of
Jesus

God's commands come

from these **2**.

What Did You Learn?

What matters most is that we love
God and that we love people.

Love and Help People

Matthew 5:44; 25:31–46
(see also John 13:35)

Jesus

wants us to treat people like we

want to be treated. It is right to give

them food to eat and water to drink.

He wants us to give people a

place to stay and clothes to

wear. When we give to other

 people, it is as if we give to Jesus! If

we take care of the sick or visit

118

people
jail
in , it's like we do those

things for too.
Jesus

What Did You Learn?

When we show love to people,
we show love to Jesus.

The Last Meal

*John 13:1—14:6 (see also
Matthew 26:20–30; Mark 14:17–26;
Luke 22:14–30)*

 knew that the time had come for

him to leave the . He went into a

room to with his disciples for the

last time. When gave them ,

he said to think of his body. When he

gave them wine, he said to think of his

blood. told them his Father's

has many rooms and he was going to

make a place ready for them in .
heaven

Then washed the of the
Jesus   feet

disciples. He said to help others like that.

What Did You Learn?

Jesus is making
a place ready for
us in heaven.

Jesus Dies to Take Away Sins

Matthew 26:53; John 15:13; 17:24;
Hebrews 9:22; 1 Peter 3:18

It hurt Jesus to be up on the cross. He

could have called  angels to save him,

but he didn't. Jesus died there to take

away the wrong things we have done. It

was the only way we could go to  heaven.

 Jesus did this because he does love

us and wants us to be with him in

 heaven someday.

122

What Did You Learn?

Jesus died on the cross so we can live with him in heaven someday.

Jesus Is Alive!

Matthew 28:1–6

After  died, his friends put his body

in a . On the **3**rd day, went to

Jesus

tomb   women

the . They were surprised because

tomb

was not there! They saw an

Jesus   angel

in front of the . The was

tomb   angel

shining brightly, and his clothes were

white. The told them, " has

angel   Jesus

risen, just as he said he would!"

124

What Did You Learn?
Jesus is alive!

Jesus Visits Many People

John 20:24–29
(see also 1 Corinthians 15:6)

 Jesus visited many people after he rose

 up from the  tomb . Thomas was

1 of the disciples. He saw with his

own eyes the holes in the hands of

 Jesus . They were from the nails

that held Jesus to the cross . Thomas

said, "My Lord and my God!" Jesus

said, "You believe because you

126

saw me." said blessed are those who believe without seeing him with their own 👀.

eyes

What Did You Learn?

We can believe in Jesus even if we don't see him with our own eyes.

Jesus Goes to Heaven

Matthew 28:16–20; Mark 16:15–16;
Luke 24:50–51 (see also Acts 1:9–11)

 told the disciples to into the
Jesus **go**

 and make disciples of all nations.
world

 said, "Whoever believes and is
Jesus

baptized will be saved." also told
Jesus

them, "I am with you always." lifted
Jesus

 his and blessed the disciples.
up **hands**

Then was taken and a hid
Jesus **up** **cloud**

him from sight. **2** came and said
angels

128

that  will come back someday, the

Jesus

same way he went ⬆ to 🌈.

up   heaven

What Did You Learn?

If we believe in Jesus, we will go to heaven someday to be with him.

The Holy Spirit Comes

Acts 1:4–5; 2:1–41

One day followers of Jesus heard a

sound from  heaven. It was like a great

 wind blowing. It filled the house. A fire

came to a stop above each of them. It did

not hurt them at all. The Holy Spirit

came into their hearts, and

they started to talk in

words they didn't know.

130

One of the disciples named Peter said,

"Everyone who calls on the name of the

Lord will be saved." **3,000** more
people

believed in that day.
Jesus

What Did You Learn?

The Holy Spirit
lives in the hearts
of people who
believe in Jesus.

Jesus Changes Saul

Acts 9:1–22

Saul was mean to followers of  Jesus

called Christians. While he looked for

Christians to put in jail, Saul saw a

bright light from heaven. He fell down and

heard Jesus ask, "Saul! Saul! Why are

you opposing me?" Saul got up from

the ground. He opened his eyes, but he

couldn't see. He was blind for **3** days.

Then a Christian put his  on Saul.

Saul opened his . He could see again! His name became Paul. After that he loved and he wrote good letters to Christians. These letters are in the .

What Did You Learn?

Jesus can change people from bad to good.

How to Live With God

Romans 3:23; 5:8; 6:23; 10:8–10

Paul wrote in the  **Bible** that everyone

has done 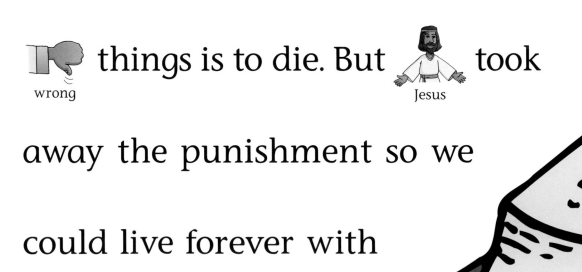 **wrong** things. Everyone has

sinned. He said no one deserves to live

with God. The punishment for doing

wrong things is to die. But **Jesus** took

away the punishment so we

could live forever with

him in **heaven**. If we

say, " is Lord" and believe that God
Jesus

raised  from the , we
Jesus up tomb

will live with God.

What Did You Learn?
Jesus is Lord!

What Love Means

1 Corinthians 13:4–8

The **Bible** says if we  **love** **people**, we

will be patient and kind. We won't be

jealous. We won't brag to **people**. We

won't be rude or think only of

ourselves. We won't get **mad**

at **people** easily. We will forget

what **people** did **wrong**. We will

not be **happy** when bad things

136

happen to . We will want them to

people

know what is and true. We will

right

protect, trust, hope, and not let

people

down. never fails.

Love

What Did You Learn?

If we love people, we will
treat them right.

John Sees Heaven

Revelation 5:13; 21:4, 21, 23; 22:5–7
(see also 1 Thessalonians 4:16–17)

God showed a man named John how

 heaven will be. It will have **12** gates

made from pearls. The main street

of the city will be gold and the

 water will be clear. There will be

no night and God will give the

 city its light. No one will be sad

there. God will wipe away every

tear from their . They will

eyes

praise to God. said he

sing

Jesus

will come soon to take believers to

!

heaven

What Did You Learn?

Heaven is a great place!

Jesus Will Come Back

Matthew 24:30–31;
1 Thessalonians 4:16–17; Revelation 22:20

Someday
Jesus
will come back. He will

come on the
clouds
of the sky. We

will hear the voice of the leader of the

angels
. And we will hear a blast from

God's
trumpet
. We will be taken
up
in

the
clouds
. We will meet
Jesus
in the

air. And we will be with him forever in

heaven
!

What Did You Learn?

Jesus is coming back to take
us with him to heaven.

Subject Index

Who Is Jesus?

QUESTION: Who is Jesus?
ANSWER: Jesus is God's Son.

Because sin came into the world when Adam and Eve disobeyed God, God asked Jesus to come to make things right again.

Jesus was born (just about 2,000 years ago), and he lived in a part of the world called Palestine.

When he was about thirty years old, he began to preach and to heal.

Three or four years later he was nailed to a cross to die. When the people who loved him went to his grave three days later, Jesus' body wasn't there.

He had come back to life, just as he said he would.

QUESTION: Where is Jesus now?
ANSWER: Jesus is in heaven with his Father.

But he has not left us alone here on earth. He sent the Holy Spirit to live with us—to make us strong when we feel like giving up,
> to help us to care about other people
> when we sometimes don't feel like it,
> to tell us that Jesus will always love us.

QUESTION: Why did Jesus have to die?
ANSWER: It was all part of God's great plan to make right what had become so wrong because of sin.

You see, we all deserve to be punished.

God loves us so much he sent Jesus to take our punishment. Because of Jesus we can know for sure that God welcomes us into his loving arms—right now and when we die and go to be with him.

QUESTION: Does Jesus love me?
ANSWER: Jesus loves you more than you can imagine.

He loves you when you cry and when you laugh; when you argue with your brother or when you've had a bad day. He loves you so much that he died for you—but he isn't still dead. He is alive, and he is loving and watching over you every day.

QUESTION: Will Jesus ever stop loving me?
ANSWER: No!

There will be times when you wonder if Jesus is really real.
There will be times when you wonder if he loves you. There will be times when you do things that you shouldn't— when you act mean to your sister or lie to your father.
But when you pray and tell Jesus that you have times when you doubt; when you pray and tell Jesus that you know you've done wrong and you want to do better— you can be sure that he will never let you down.
He will love you your whole life long, and you will live with him forever.

QUESTION: How do I know I'm a Christian?
ANSWER: There are many signs.

When you love Jesus with all the love you can give, when you know deep down that Jesus loves you, when you believe he died to forgive your sins, when you want to live for Jesus—those are good signs that help you know you are a Christian.
Sure, you're going to fail sometimes. But, you see, God's love for you is so great that it covers those times when you fail. He sees deep into your heart. He knows your desire to live for him, and *he loves you.*

Who Made This Book?

Author: Tracy Harrast
Project Management and editorial: Catherine DeVries
Interior Art and Cover Art: Garry Colby
Interior Design: Jody DeNeef and Catherine DeVries
Art Direction: Jody Langley
Typesetting: Jody DeNeef
Cover Design: Cynthia Tobey
Printing: R.R. Donnelley & Sons, Roanoke, VA

10 Commandments

 afraid

 angel

 ark

 army

 boat

 bread

 camels

 children

 city

 donkey

 down

 drink

 eat

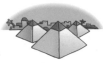 Egypt

 flowers

 frog

 garden

 giant

 go

 ground

 inn

 Israelites

 jail

 Jesus

 king

 moon

 mountain

 nails

 net

 night

 rock

 roof

 sad

 salt

 servant

 star

 statue

 stone

 stop

 storm

 tree

 trumpet

 up

 walk

 wall